UNUSUAL GRAVESTONES

Martin and Claire Nicholson

St Pauls Cemetery, Coventry, Warwickshire

Competitive grave-hunting for beginners –
how to rate your discoveries.

ACKNOWLEDGEMENTS

We would like to thank our daughters Hazel and Sally, our friend David and our siblings Stephen, Jane and Helen for their contributions to the survey work that underpinned this book.

Copyright © 2015 by Martin Nicholson

Martin and Claire Nicholson
Church Stretton, Shropshire

Email – newbinaries@yahoo.co.uk

INTRODUCTION

This book is a product of the authors' survey of graveyards and cemeteries that began in 2008. The survey began out of an interest in looking for the gravestones of centenarians, but soon expanded to include other gravestones that were of interest for different reasons. All these gravestones were photographed, together with a general view of the church or cemetery and the results are available on a website www.grave-mistakes.info.

The history of most churches is well documented and it is often available online. There are also continuing projects to make parish registers available online.

However almost no churches offer detailed guides to the inscriptions on the gravestones in their churchyards. Occasionally a study has been made of a single churchyard by an enthusiastic local person, but no-one seems to have made studies of all the burial sites of larger areas. The development of the digital camera has now made projects such as this survey possible.

The survey made by the authors began when they lived in Northamptonshire and continues now that they live in Shropshire. The majority of sites they have visited have been local to their homes, but they also visit sites whenever they are in other parts of the country.

Rarity scale.

After viewing millions of gravestones, the authors now have a good understanding of the types of features that make a gravestone unusual. For example, a person whose first visit to a graveyard was in a coal-mining area might conclude that gravestones which refer to death in mining accidents are quite common. This is not so. Therefore a rarity-scoring system has been devised which attempts to quantify the likelihood of finding gravestones with particular features. It is hoped that grave-hunters will then be better able to appreciate how rare the gravestones that they discover are.

The authors estimate that they have photographed well under 1% of the gravestones that they have looked at, so they do not want readers to think that it has been easy to find all those illustrated in this book! The fun of the chase though does make a good day out!

We have decided that the top score of 100 points is awarded to gravestones of which we have only ever seen 1 or 2 examples.

TIPS FOR SUCCESSFUL GRAVE-HUNTING.

1. Choose a sunny day – your photographs will look so much nicer.
2. Do not visit graveyards alone. Many churches are isolated, and the furthest corners of the sites may not be visited by anyone for very long periods. Some urban cemeteries may be favoured by "undesirables".
3. Wear sensible footwear. The ground surface can be very uneven and long grass can be very wet even in summer.
4. Use a good-quality camera for photographing the church or whole site and your gravestone discoveries. Set the clock on the camera to the correct time.
5. Take a notebook to keep records if you visit more than one site and record the time to aid in subsequent identification of your photographs.
6. Do not miss out that last gravestone in the corner and always look over walls and hedges or across the road for churchyard extensions.
7. Always try the door of the church and keep a record of those that are locked for a possible further visit. Sometimes there is a notice giving the location of the key. Do not expect that only grand churches have grand interior monuments – sometimes quite ordinary-looking small rural churches can have a spectacular interior memorial or monument.
8. Take some money to buy the leaflet about the history of the church, but do not expect it to have significant information about the graveyard.
9. Philips Street Atlases have every church marked and are large scale. Many rural churches are well hidden and in very isolated positions.
10. In large urban cemeteries it can be helpful to sketch the site plan near the entrance and then cross off each area as you survey it. Do not expect it to be a quick task to look at every gravestone at such a site. The authors have spent 3 or 4 hours at a large cemetery and have had to revisit it on another day to complete their survey.
11. Be respectful to mourners and if the vicar is in the church ask his permission for photography inside the church. You may have to pay for a photography permit inside a cathedral or other large church that is popular with tourists.
12. The people who maintain churchyards are often volunteers, so be appreciative of their work – remember that everyone likes a compliment!
13. At home, internet research will often yield interesting details about churches and also about "incidents" noted on gravestones.
14. Do not delay – gravestones are deteriorating and may be either illegible or removed altogether next year.

Graves of old people - In theory the age at death should be one of the easiest facts to discover from a gravestone. Unfortunately this is not always the case. In many graveyards some stones have been so eroded by years of exposure to the weather that the text has become unreadable. Also many stones do not include full details of the dates of birth and death so it is impossible for the age of the deceased to be determined.

The most common example of this problem is when only the year of birth and death are included in the inscription. "John Smith, 1890 to 1990" could indicate that John had celebrated his 100th birthday but he might have been still aged 99 when he died.

When the year of birth or death has been abbreviated to just 2 digits – for example "John Smith 00 to 01" - there may be no way of telling if John died very young or very old. In such cases it is always best to assume that death occurred at a young age.

From the start of the survey reaching the age of 100 was the minimum qualification to qualify for a photograph and a permanent record in the published archive. A centenarian is a person who lives to or beyond their 100th birthday and 0.1% of centenarians go on to become super-centenarians by reaching the age of 110. Most of the people we have recorded as having reached the age of 100 have died in recent decades, so for this reason our rarity chart not only takes into account the age at death but also the year of death.

The graves of the oldest man and the oldest lady we have found while doing our survey.

Sources - Saffron Hill Cemetery, Leicester and St Mary the Virgin, Burghill, Herefordshire

Age at death	Died 1960 onwards		Died before 1960	
	Female	Male	Female	Male
100	1 point	5 points	5 points	25 points
101	2	10	10	50
102	3	15	15	100
103	5	25	25	100
104	10	40	40	100
105	15	50	50	100
106	25	100	100	100
107	40	100	100	100
108	50	100	100	100
109+	100	100	100	100

Although modern graveyards and crematoria are the most prolific source of memorials to centenarians, socio-economic factors make a significant difference to the success rate achieved by grave hunters. In areas of economic and social deprivation disproportionately few people reach the age of 100. The most extreme example of this was the very large Shire Lodge Cemetery in Corby where we failed to find a single example of a person reaching the age of 100.

Much rarer than "just" being a centenarian is being a member of the very elite group of people who lived in three centuries. The vast majority of such people have lived in the 19th, 20th and 21st centuries but Anna Maria Brown died in 1904 at the age of 105.

Source - Market Harborough Cemetery, Leicestershire

Source - St Non, Llanerchaeron, Ceredigion, Wales

Annie Florence Edgar lived in three centuries and experienced six reigning monarchs. The grave of Anna Maria Brown is "worth" a lot more than that of Annie Edgar because dying at 105 in 1904 is much more unusual than dying at 105 in 2004.

Life span	Female	Male
1890s to 2000s	75 points	100 points
1790s to 1900s	100	100

Source - St Clement, St Clement, Cornwall

John and Mary Benny both died when "considerably above 80 years of age".

Source - St Mary Magdalene, Horton, Northamptonshire

1934 wasn't a leap year so there wasn't a 29th February!

Two "near misses" – 99 years and 360 days plus 99 years and 364 days.

**Sources - St Peter, Adderley, Shropshire
and London Road Cemetery, Stony Stratford, Buckinghamshire**

Age not known	40 points
Impossible dates	100
"Near misses"	25

Young people - Older graveyards are the best source of graves of infants dying before the age of one year. The infant mortality rate, expressed in terms of the number dying per 1,000 live births, was 140 in 1900, 35 in 1950 and 4.8 in 2009. It is by no means unusual to find the deaths of several infant children reported on the same memorial. The most poignant example of this that we have found dates back to the middle of the eighteenth century.

Source - St Augustine, Droitwich Spa, Worcestershire

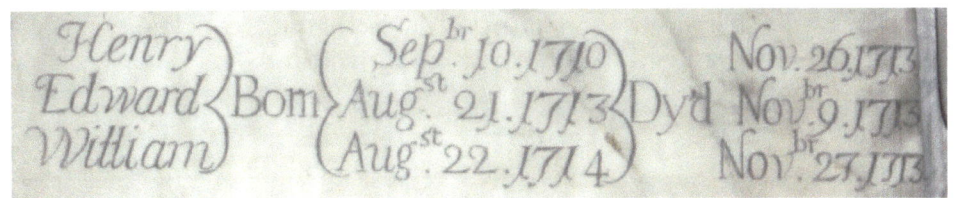

Source - St Kenelm, Clifton-upon-Teme, Worcestershire

Sometimes the quoted dates of birth and death don't make sense. In this example William appears to have died nine months before he was born!

Source - Barnsley Cemetery, Barnsley, South Yorkshire

There was a small area of the cemetery set aside for stillborn and neonatal babies. The whole area reflects great credit on all involved in the project.

Marriage - Many gravestones report the details of married couples. In many cases, particularly when both members are elderly, they die within a year or two of each other. At the other extreme, and in many ways much sadder, are the people who experienced over 50 years as a widow or widower.

Elizabeth (61) and Edward Easthope (62) died on consecutive days in January 1894.

Note how the final word "divided" has been engraved as "devided".

Source - St Swithin, Clunbury, Shropshire

A widow for 67 years.

A widower for 64 years.

**Sources - St John's Cemetery, Worcester, Worcestershire
and Tewksbury Cemetery, Tewksbury, Gloucestershire**

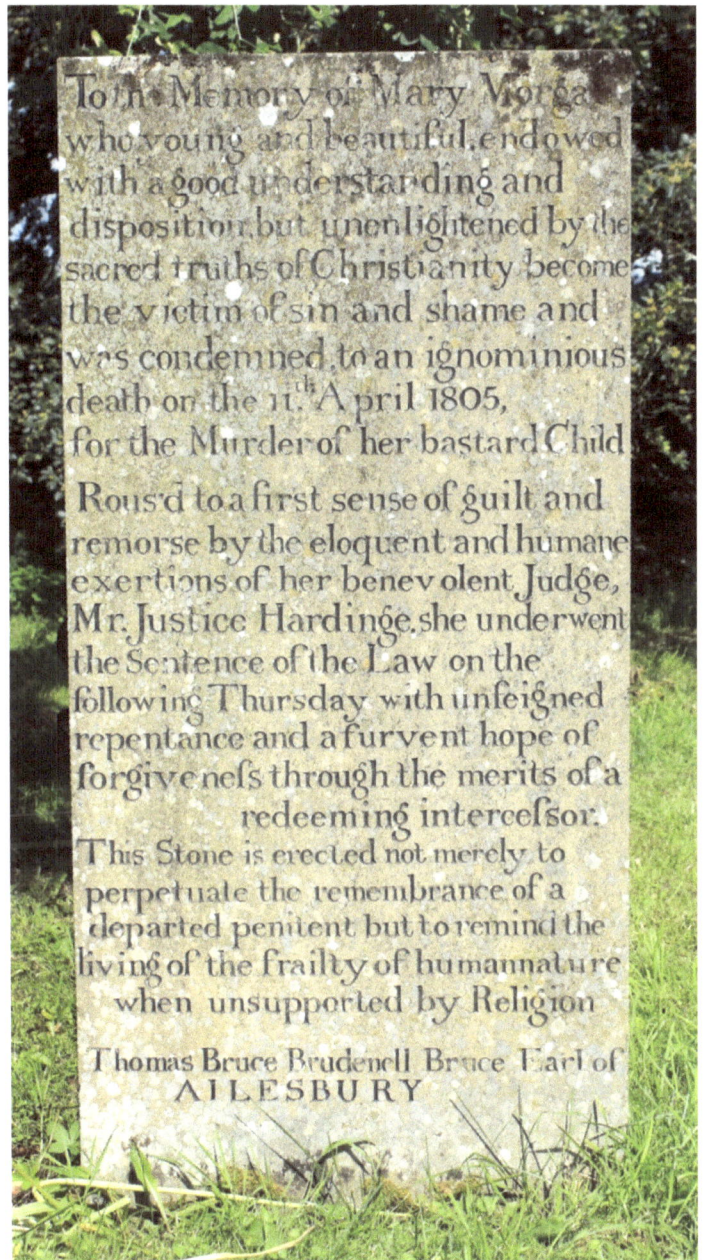

for the Murder of her bastard Child

To the Memory of Mary Morgan
who young and beautiful, endowed
with a good understanding and
disposition but unenlightened by the
sacred truths of Christianity became
the victim of sin and shame and
was condemned to an ignominious
death on the 11th April 1805,
for the Murder of her bastard Child

Rous'd to a first sense of guilt and
remorse by the eloquent and humane
exertions of her benevolent Judge,
Mr. Justice Hardinge, she underwent
the Sentence of the Law on the
following Thursday with unfeigned
repentance and a furvent hope of
forgivenefs through the merits of a
redeeming intercefsor.
This Stone is erected not merely to
perpetuate the remembrance of a
departed penitent but to remind the
living of the frailty of humannature
when unsupported by Religion

Thomas Bruce Brudenll Bruce Earl of
AILESBURY

Source - St Andrew, Presteigne, Powys, Wales

13

Murder victim

PC William Davies, 43, died from injuries suffered whilst trying to make an arrest in Montgomery in 1903. The police then evicted his wife and four children from the family home two weeks after his death.

Heather Arnold, 59, was found guilty in 1987 of murdering Jeanne Sutcliffe and her eight-month-old daughter in Westbury, Wiltshire.

**Sources - St Nicholas, Montgomery, Powys
and Westbury Cemetery, Westbury, Wiltshire**

The "sudden explosion of a fowling piece"

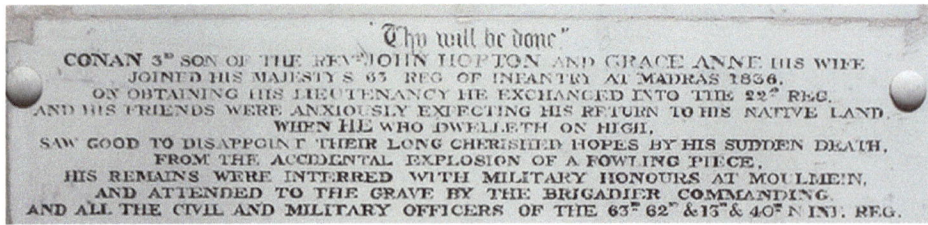

Source - St James, Canon Frome, Herefordshire

Illness and infection

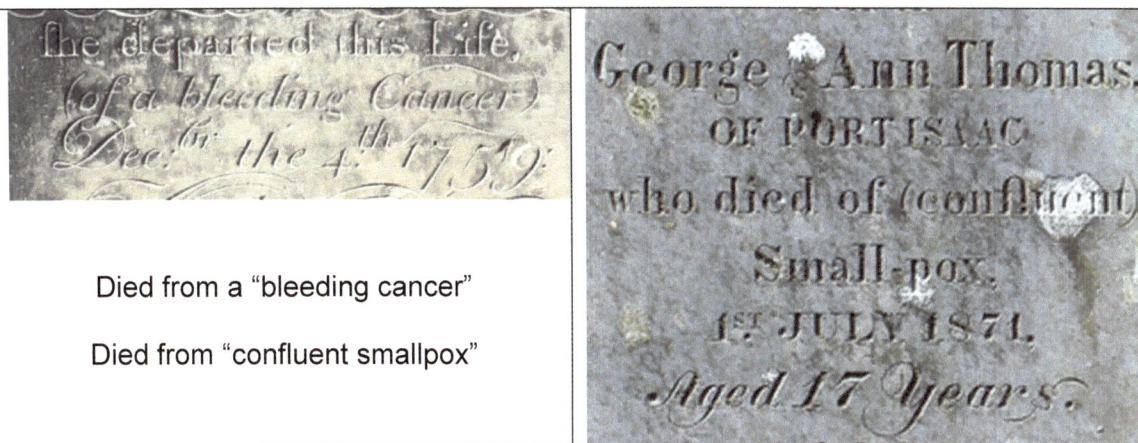

Died from a "bleeding cancer"

Died from "confluent smallpox"

**Sources - All Saints, Long Whatton, Leicestershire
and St Endelienta, St Endellion, Cornwall**

Killed at work

Source - St John the Baptist, Bromsgrove, Worcestershire

Thomas Scaife and Joseph Rutherford both worked for the Birmingham and Gloucester Railway and were killed when the boiler on a steam locomotive exploded at Bromsgrove on 10th November 1840. Scaife was killed at once but Rutherford died the next day.

Drowned

Five boys, including two brothers, were accidentally drowned in one accident in 1901.

Peter Oliver was drowned when he was only 2 years and 3 months old.

Sources - Kilmartin Cemetery, Argyll and Bute, Scotland and Hengoed Cemetery, Hengoed, Shropshire

Drowned or presumed drowned at sea

Source - Barnoon Cemetery, St Ives, Cornwall

Died in an air-crash

**Sources - St James, Kimbolton, Herefordshire
and Holy Cross, Bobbington, Staffordshire**

Ernest Harris was 1 of the 50 people killed in an air-crash in Malta in 1956. The accident was caused by a combination of engine failure and pilot error.

Prince William of Gloucester was a member of the British Royal Family, a grandson of George V. He died due to pilot error during an air-show.

Died in a road accident

Source - Tewkesbury Cemetery, Tewkesbury, Gloucestershire

A mother, father and two young children were all killed in a road accident.

Causes of death (Civilian war dead) - .

Source - Dervaig Cemetery, Isle of Mull, Scotland

It was so sad to think that these brave sailors were buried without anybody knowing their names. It says "Known unto God" on the gravestones - I certainly hope so.

From left to right - unknown 21st August 1940, unknown 15th September 1940, W D Davies S.S. Bibury 2nd September 1940, unknown 12th October 1940, unknown ? October 1940.

Causes of death (Armed forces)

Source - The Cemetery and Mausoleum, Weston Under Lizard, Staffordshire - "He knew not fear" seems a very fitting epitaph to put on the grave of the Hon. R. O. B. Bridgeman who died on active service.

Neville Martyn died at Malta in 1892 from "Malta Fever" or brucellosis.

Maurice Albert died in a Japanese Prisoner of War camp.

Sources - St Buriana, St Buryan, Cornwall and St Peter, Arnesby, Leicestershire

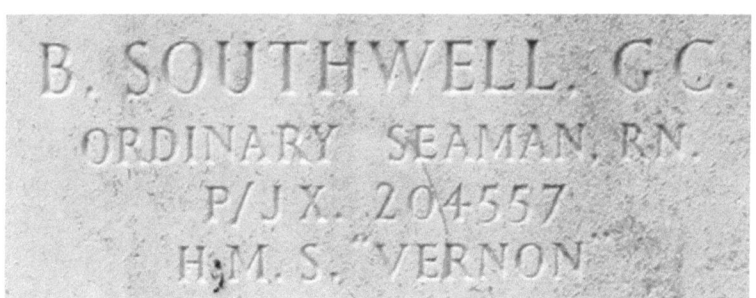

Source - Gilroes Cemetery, Leicester, Leicestershire

The George Cross (GC) is the highest civil decoration of the United Kingdom. Bennett Southwell was killed carrying out bomb disposal work during the London Blitz.

War Memorials

Source - St Peter and St Paul, Whitney-on-Wye, Herefordshire

A round-headed chamfered doorway has been blocked and now contains a timber First World War memorial. Alan Lewis was a Lance-Corporal in the 6th Battalion, The Northamptonshire Regiment, when he was awarded the Victoria Cross.

Source - St John the Baptist, Stokesay, Shropshire

This is an impressive war memorial despite the soldier looking distinctly middle-aged.

Civilian deaths

Executed	100 points
Murdered	100
Named illness	10
Killed at work	2
Drowned	2
Presumed drowned	15
Air accident	25
Road accident	2

Military deaths

Civilian war victim	25 points
Prisoner of War	10
George Cross or Victoria Cross	40
Outdoor wooden war memorial	50
War memorial statue	25

Design and inscription features

Unusual raw material	
Glass	100 points
Stainless steel	50
Home made	10
Occupation	
Physician	5 points
Servant	2
Lion Tamer	100
Unusual shape	20
Uninformative	15
Unusual names	10
Last words	50

We invite readers to award themselves points for other rarities. The "Lion Tamer" is not imaginary – we have seen a gravestone for "The foremost lion tamer of his age" at St Philip, Penn Fields, Wolverhampton, West Midlands.

Design Features – Raw material used A review of the web sites of monumental masons not only gives a clear idea of what is standard practice in modern cemeteries but, more usefully for the grave hunter, enables unusual designs and raw materials to be identified.

Granite is popular and comes in many colours. Sometimes there is insufficient contrast between the colour of the stone and the lettering and this can make the memorial very difficult to read. White Marble and limestone are more expensive but suffer far less from the problem of unreadable inscriptions. Our favourite raw material is slate because we have seen many slate gravestones that are over 200 years old and as readable as the day they were erected.

Source - Kingsthorpe Cemetery, Northampton, Northamptonshire

Design Features – Occupation

Lifeboat Coxswain

Gate Keeper and Messenger at the Aberystwyth Union Workhouse

Gem and Seal Stone Engraver

Rope Maker

Source - Aberystwyth Cemetery, Aberystwyth, Ceredigion

Design Features – Shape

Source - Chingford Mount Cemetery, Greater London

**Sources - St Pauls Cemetery, Coventry, Warwickshire
and Crownhill Crematorium, Milton Keynes, Buckinghamshire**

Design Features – Unhelpful and uninformative inscriptions

Source - St Michael and All Angels, Cofton Hackett, Worcestershire

Source - Southam Road Cemetery, Banbury, Oxfordshire

Design Features – Unusual names

At the start of the Victorian era the ten most common first names for girls accounted for 67% of all names. In order the top 10 were Mary, Elizabeth, Sarah, Ann, Jane, Hannah, Emma, Eliza, Ellen and Harriet. By 1898 the 10 most common names only made up 36% of all names.

Examples of unusual names we have found in our home county of Shropshire include Sophronia, Druscilla, Trypheana and Lamartine:

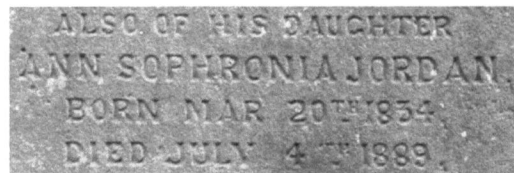

Source – Bridgnorth Cemetery

Source – Broseley Cemetery

Source – St Peter, Cound

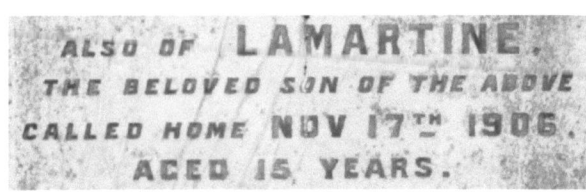

Source – Leintwardine Cemetery

"Last words"

Source - All Saints, Claverley, Shropshire

His last words were "Psalm 23".

Source - St Michael and All Angels, Cofton Hackett, Worcestershire

Her last words were "To Heaven, Mamma, To Heaven, Mamma, To Heaven, Mamma"

Mistakes

Errors – Additions and deletions

Source - St Andrew, Church Aston, Shropshire

The year of death and the age have both been altered

Errors – Punctuation

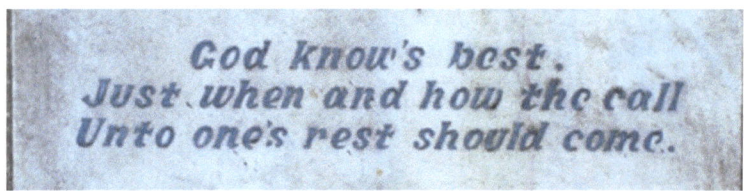

Source - St Mary, Abberley, Worcestershire

God knows best

Errors – Spelling

Source - St Laurence, Church Stretton, Shropshire

Cherished not cherishd

Source - St Margaret of Antioch, Crick, Northamptonshire

How do you spell George?

Errors – Spelling (homophone)

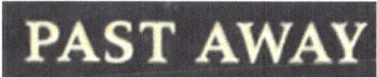

Source - St Mary Magdalene, Penley, Wrexham

It should read "passed away".

Additions and deletions	3 points
Punctuation	10
Spelling	5
Homophones	40

Disrespectful sites

Source - All Saints, Mollington, Oxfordshire

Source - St Lawrence, Stretton Grandison, Herefordshire

Against fierce opposition St Lawrence, Stretton Grandison has been awarded first prize in the "least respectful churchyard in Herefordshire" competition. The Bishop of Hereford has been informed of this cultural vandalism. Far too often the people responsible for the routine maintenance of churchyards are citing "financial constraints" or are using the "but it is also a nature reserve" excuse to justify allowing many graves to become both inaccessible and overgrown.

www.ingramcontent.com/pod-product-compliance
Lightning Source LLC
Chambersburg PA
CBHW060805290526
45792CB00005BA/1529